Croquet Guide and Official Rules Governing the Game

CROQUET GUIDE

AND

OFFICIAL RULES GOVERNING THE GAME

AS ADOPTED BY THE

NATIONAL AMERICAN CROQUET ASSOCIATION

※

AUTHORIZED EDITION

※

Revised and Corrected by the National Association up to 1897

※

PUBLISHED FOR THE ASSOCIATION BY THE
AMERICAN SPORTS PUBLISHING COMPANY
241 BROADWAY, NEW YORK
Copyright, 1897, by American Sports Publishing Co

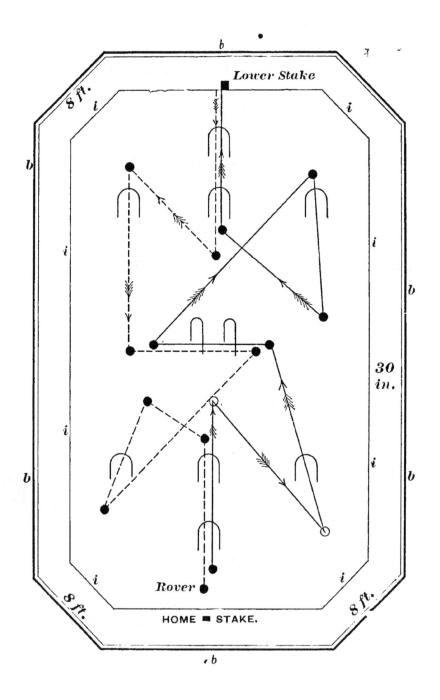

DESCRIPTION OF GROUNDS.

On the opposite page will be found the plan of a ground as adopted by the National Association, the dimensions of which are as follows: Length, 72 ft.; width, 36 ft.; corner pieces 8 ft. long, inside measurements, with a line denoting the boundary of the field 30 in. from the inside of the border. The stakes or post to be 1 in. in diameter and $1\frac{1}{2}$ in. high, situated outside of the above mentioned line at the centre of the width of the field. The first wicket to be 7 ft. from the stake; the second, 7 ft. from the first, on a line extending through the middle of the field; the side arches to be 6 ft. 3 in. from the border, on a line with the second arch from each stake; the cage or double wicket in the centre to be 18 in. long and $3\frac{3}{8}$ in. between the wires, and set at right angles with a line drawn from stake to stake; the other eight arches to be $3\frac{1}{2}$ in. between the wires.

The border, $b, b, b,$ is best when made of some hard wood that will not warp, not smaller than 4 x 6 in., laid flat to serve as a cushion for carom shots; this timber or border should be beveled $\frac{1}{2}$ in., making it measure 6 in. wide on top, $5\frac{1}{2}$ in. wide on the bottom and 4 inches high, which will prevent balls from jumping up or off the ground when used as a cushion.

The boundary line, $i, i, i,$ is simply a light line drawn 30 in. from or inside the border to indicate the boundary of the field (See Rule 38). This line can be easily made with a marker, having a small projecting nail point, drawn around the ground and held against the border, securing uniform distance.

CROQUET.

Croquet is a comparatively modern game. It has not the weight of years on its side to increase love and regard for it.

The name seems to indicate France as its origin, and it is said to have been brought from there to Ireland, thence to England.

Public match games were played in England as long ago as 1867. As a lawn game it became exceedingly popular, and the formation of the "All England's Croquet Club" was succeeded by several annual contests for Championship at Wimbledon.

When introduced in this country, it was characterized as a game, simple and almost devoid of opportunities for the display of any very great skill. The game was also modified; the number of arches increased, their positions changed, and the size of the grounds diminished.

The finest playing at that time, and till within a few years, was upon lawns with closely mown grass and generally level surface ; but now the scientific player prepares a ground better adapted to his needs, and the exhibition of his skill.

Although much genuine pleasure and excellent exercise can be obtained from a so-called sod ground. yet for delicacy and accuracy of play and exercise of sometimes marvelous skill, the modern ground is made a perfectly level, hard-rolled, sanded field.

All Tournament games must be played on a ground of this kind.

It has ceased, therefore, to be a so-called lawn-sport among scientific players. The sanded surface gathers no dampness as evening hours approach (the most common time for play, especially in warm weather), and the caution against damp feet on the dew-covered grass is unnecessary.

It is very little trouble to maintain a good ground when once properly prepared, and the natural soil in most localities serves as an excellent basis for the top-

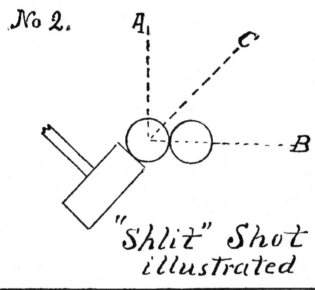

"Shlit" Shot illustrated

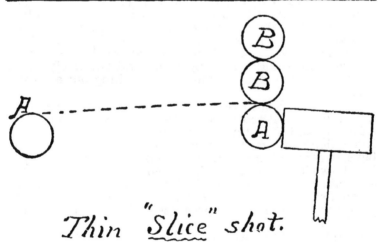

Thin "Slice" shot.
B being only slightly displaced

soil, which should be sifted if necessary to free it from stones and pebbles, and covered after hard rolling with a very slight sprinkling of fine sand.

We would by no means discourage lawn-croquet. It is from the ranks of excellent lawn players that our best scientific players have come, and lawn playing will foster a love for the game, which, after all, is the principal thing. Very few people, comparatively, have ever seen a really scientifically made ground. Those who believe themselves to be expert lawn players are greatly surprised at the greater opportunity for pleasure and skill afforded upon a nicely sanded level field.

There is no other field game that can compare with Croquet as a test for good temper, forbearance, and that prince of manly qualities, fairness.

We have known characters vastly improve by courteous companionship and prevailing geniality on the Croquet ground. The old-fashioned wordy strifes and contentions, cherishing and continuing ill-feeling, are unknown, and aside from the beneficial physical advantages, these features must also be regarded in taking stock of the benefits of Croquet.

Croquet needs no special dress. The absence of excessive physical exertion is suited to those who would, if compelled to change suits, take no exercise at all, and they can return to business or any avocation after an hour of Croquet with linen and clothes none worse for their effort, and with an exhilaration that out-door exercises invariably secure. It is especially adapted to sedentary persons, and those in mature life to whom the vigorous roughness of base-ball and the lively skirmishing of lawn tennis would be anything but a pleasure.

An organized club reduces the items of expense to a minimum, and it requires but two to play the game.

In England lawn tennis has almost displaced it; but it has done so because prepared grounds were, we believe, never used there. Lawn playing only was indulged in. Lawn Tennis is a rival in this country, though not at all similar; but we doubt if all its attractions have ever persuaded one whose faith has been firmly fixed, and whose skill has made fair progress in Croquet, to give up his first love.

Croquet is as scientific as billiards. There is a greater field (literally as well as otherwise) for strategy, the exercise of deliberate judgment, nerve, coolness and bold-

No. 3.

"Wiring", or hiding, next ball. "B" by direct Roquet-Croquet, (done by usual stroke of mallet)

ness of play in Croquet than in billiards, much as some may question the truthfulness of the assertion. The eye and the hand become trained. Lawn Tennis calls for muscular action in immediate response to counter-play. Judgment must be instantaneous and muscular movements rapid and fatiguing. Croquet stands in strong contrast with its deliberate strokes, its moderate exercise and non-fatiguing efforts even when prolonged. It is richly deserving of increased interest.

The high degree of skill of which the game by the introduction of narrow arches, hard rubber balls, and the most approved implements of play has been made capable, prevents it from being regarded as fit only for children. The average age of the contestants at the last two Tournaments of the National Association at Norwich, was over forty years.

The chief points of excellence in Croquet may be enumerated as follows:

First. Accuracy in croqueting or making one ball hit another from the blow of the mallet. Here the accurate eye and the trained hand are needed, for at a distance of 10 feet a ball $3\frac{1}{4}$ inches in diameter subtends a very small angle, and a very small divergence of the line of direction of the impinging mallet will cause the struck ball to go wide of its desired course.

Second. Ability to take position in front of Arches so as to pass through them successfully, for the Arches being only $3\frac{7}{8}$ inches wide give little chance of passing through to a ball of $3\frac{1}{4}$ inches when in a "wild position."

Third. "Wiring" or "staking" an adversary's ball so as to leave no ball "open" or "exposed." This is done sometimes from a distance of fifteen or twenty feet; and fourth and greatest of all, is good generalship, for without this all excellence attained in the three preceding points will be manifested in vain in a hard-fought game. Closely associated with the first, is the ability to "drive" or "block" the ball at a certain angle to reach a position desired. This will be attempted only when the balls are near together, for at a long range roquet only is attempted. It is possible also that "jump shooting" ought to be added to these, for this, at first thought seemingly impossible method of play, is a special feature with some players, and not infrequently they are relieved from an otherwise inextricable position by a timely jump shot, by which a ball from a peculiar downward

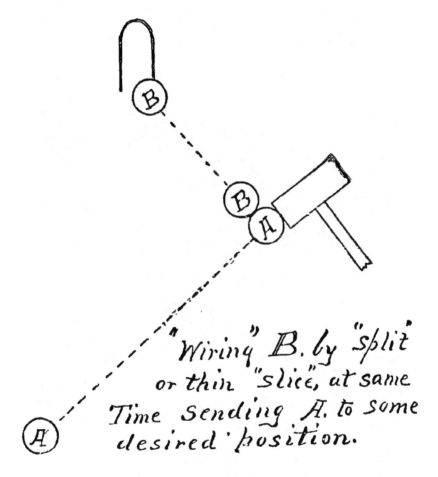

stroke of the mallet may be made to pass over one or more intervening arches and "capture" a ball supposed to be safe from all danger. [See Fig. No. 6.]

The National Association meets in Norwich on the Monday preceding the third Tuesday in August, and any one lacking enthusiasm can here be cheaply and fully "enthused." People living in or near New York can find grounds corner of Eighty-eighth Street and Madison Avenue, also at Mariners' Harbor, Staten Island, and at Matawan, New Jersey.

Philadelphia has fine, well-kept grounds at Twenty-second and Brown Streets. Danbury, New London and Middletown, Conn., Northampton, Springfield, Shelburne Falls and Leominster, Mass., boast of excellent grounds and excellent players. Cottage City, Martha's Vineyard, has ten grounds for summer play. Washington, D. C., Wilmington, Del., and Norfolk, Va., have caught the croquet spirit in earnest; Los Angeles and Palo Alto, Cal., and Albion, N. Y., are not a whit behind. Asbury Grove, Mass., has most excellent grounds and fine players at that delightful summer resort. Trenton, N. J., also has enthusiastic players. The Martha's Vineyard club has rubber borders and no slope inside. The grounds are the most artistic and expensive in the country, and do much to foster the croquet spirit. Permanent grounds have been secured at Norwich, and a building for the use of players at national tournaments has been completed and paid for.

The Western clubs have never been represented at the National Association, though urgent invitations have been given them to do so. Their style of play is a little different, but it would be easily possible to unify all existing games of the so-called "loose" or "tight" croquet, and this ought to be done.

At Elyria, Ohio, they have covered grounds and their players cannot be excelled. But Norwich has been called the genuine Mecca for the lovers of Croquet. Easily reached, with an old love for the game, with players celebrated for their geniality, hospitality and skill, the Rose City of New England is especially a haven of delight, and the third week of August is looked forward to by Croquetists with the eagerness and unconcealed pleasure of children looking forward to the joys and festivities of Christmastide.

The game of Croquet should be played on ground as nearly level as possible, in size 36 x 72 feet. The surface should be well-rolled dirt, lightly sanded to hold the balls. While the game may be played on turf, all national match or tournament games shall be played on a dirt or "made" ground.

In all prize tournament games the wickets shall be not more than three and one-half inches in width, and the "cage" or center wicket shall be not more than three and three-eighths inches in width by eighteen inches in length. This wicket shall be set in the center of the field with its long axis at right angles with a line drawn from stake to stake. It is so situated to make the wiring of balls more difficult.

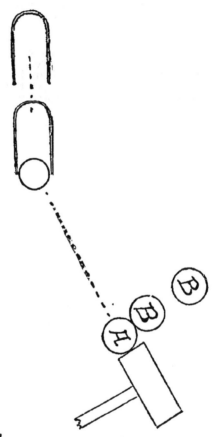

No. 5.

Getting "Position" in the "Cage" by "split" Shot.

The wickets should be sunk into the ground six or eight inches or set in blocks of wood, buried under the surface to insure stability.

The MALLETS [see Rule 8] may be made of boxwood, seven or seven and one-half inches long by two and one-fourth to two and one-half inches in diameter, and the handle from eight to fifteen inches in length, as best suits the player. Individual taste has caused a great variety of mallets. The steel (or brass) tube is becoming increasingly popular, mainly from its strength to endure hard blows. It has a hard and a soft rubber end, being filled with wood driven in hard. The best balls are of hard rubber; and in a.l National Association games they shall be of hard rubber, three and one-fourth inches in diameter. They can be easily painted, by using a preparation of shellac dissolved in alcohol, mixing with Chinese vermillion for red, Prussian blue and zinc or flake white for blue, and zinc or flake white for white. Thus painted they will dry in a few minutes and wear for several days

No. 6

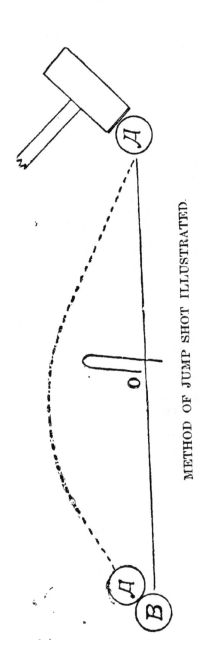

METHOD OF JUMP SHOT ILLUSTRATED.

TO THE BEGINNER.

In this, as in every other game, there are certain general principles which should guide one in his play. Before referring to these we will notice 1st, mallets, and 2d, the position taken in the use of the mallet. A mallet should be from 7 to 8 inches in length by about 2½ inches in diameter, with handle from 12 to 18 inches long. The size and weight should be that which, after trial, the player likes the best.

As regards position in striking, let every man be a law unto himself. My way might not suit you, and your way would not suit me; yet while occupying very different positions, we may aim and execute with equal accuracy. Do not be too long in your aim; a quick stroke after getting your line between two balls is generally the most accurate; but there is one point that all must observe if the ball is to hit the mark: after getting your line of aim, and your mallet resting ready for the stroke, keep your eyes fixed on your own ball. Any deviation from this rule, either for short or long shots, will end in failure.

And now as to a few general principles to be observed:

First. Keep your own balls together, and separate those of your adversary.

Second. Keep with you or your partner the "innocent" or last played ball of your adversary.

Third. Keep the "guilty" or next playing ball of your adversary wired as much as possible.

Fourth. When you can make no further run, give your partner the best set up you can.

Fifth. Do not play for the guilty ball when, if you miss, you give him a chance better than he has before.

Sixth. If you have but a poor chance to make a run, set up the balls for your partner.

Seventh. In making a run, provide as much as possible for points ahead. Do not leave balls behind you if you can avoid it.

To bring out the points of a game, let us illustrate:

Having scored for first shot (see Rule 7 for method of opening the game), and Blue having won, the balls are then placed at the four corners of the field nearest the centre, and Blue plays at White, probably missing, but resting near his partner, Red; Black follows with most likely the same result Then Red plays on Blue, croqueting in as near the first arch as he can, and getting, if possible, a drive on White, so as to wire it from Blue, between the lower stake and wicket Then Red plays on Black with the hope of being able to make some wickets, but should there not be a good show he croquets in to Blue, and leaves a "set-up" for his partner by resting near the first wicket. This method is generally attempted when the first two shots fail to strike a ball. If White has but one ball to play for the length of the field, his chances of missing are so great that it is preferable to remain at the lower end of the field. He thus forces Blue to come after him by croquet from a ball near him, or play with only his partner and the "guilty" or next playing ball. Blue now has his balls to aid him in making a run. If he feels capable of managing it, he should roquet Black, croquet to White, and bring it into his field of play, then make his first arch off Red. He now has all the balls in the field. He plays on Red and sends it toward the center arch; then on Black, sending it towards the third arch; then on White, making his second arch. He should endeavor to have a drive on White now to the center, leaving it there, shoving Red to third, making third off Black, keeping it near the wicket. Here he should wire it by leaving it directly behind the third arch and then drive Red towards center, getting his position for the center arch off White. If he succeeds in this and makes the arch, he goes on securely and confidently, for Black is not likely to do him any harm, even if he fails in his arch.

This illustrates his successful play far enough, indicating what he should do throughout the game. If he fails at the center, Black then plays to the lower part of the field, or to an upper corner if he must, and Red now plays. There are now two courses open for Red, either to try to make a run, or assist Blue. If Blue is in position, he should prefer the latter course, especially if other balls are not in the field, affording him an opportunity for a drive. He either puts Blue through the center, or where it can easily go through, then wires White and rests where Blue can reach him in passing through the cage. White should now get as far away as possible, leaving Blue only the Red ball to assist him in making a further run. If Black is on the line, White should get as near as possible.

If Red has brought Black into the field, then White plays to the upper end of the field. Blue goes through, continues his run with two balls, and at the stake gets White back into the field, wiring or staking Black at his first convenient opportunity. If Blue fails and Black or White succeed in getting the balls, the same general plan is carried out. It is a good rule not to try to make the third arch unless you have a set-up for the cage, except it be necessary to do so in order to get out of danger. If you are for the cage, and lose the balls, it is much more difficult to get started for another run than if you were for some other arch. As caroms from the border count, balls should be wired if possible to prevent even carom shots.

TERMS USED IN CROQUET.

To Roquet.—To hit with one's own ball another ball for the first time.

To Croquet.—To place player's ball against the roqueted ball and then striking his own ball, moving both.

Carom.—A rebounding from an arch, a stake, or the border.

In Play.—A ball is in play so long as points are made, or balls hit in accordance with the rules.

Points.—See Rule 23.

Dead Ball.—A ball on which the player has played since making a point. It is then *dead* to the player till he makes another point or has another turn.

Direct Shot—Roquet.—This is a direct shot, whether the ball in passing to its destination does or does not carom from a wire, or a stake or the border.

Drive or Block—English "Rush"—A roquet played so as to send the object ball to some desired spot.

Cut.—To drive the object ball to a desired position, by causing player's ball to hit it on one side.

Run or Break.—The making of a number of points in the same turn.

Set Up.—To locate the balls so as to afford facility for making the next point or run.

Wiring.—To leave the balls so that the next finds a wire between his ball and the object ball.

Object Ball.—The ball at which the player aims.

Jump Shot.—Striking the ball so as to make it jump over any obstacle between it and the object aimed at. To do this, the ball should be struck with considerable force on the top just back of the center

Guilty or Danger Ball.—The next played on the adversary's side.

Innocent Ball.—The last played ball of the adversary.

Rover.—A ball that has made all the points except the last.

Tight Croquet.—Is holding with the hand or foot the ball placed against another for the sake of croquet, thus allowing only the latter to be moved.

Loose Croquet.—Is striking a ball when it is in contact with another, where it has been placed for the purpose of croquet, thus moving both balls.

Scoring.—See Rule 7.

CROQUET RULES.

NOTE.—The following Rules, though adapted and adopted for Loose Croquet, are, nevertheless, used by the most prominent clubs of the country as authority in *Tight Croquet*. Some rulings are to be construed as referring only to Loose Croquet. But of these there can be no doubt, from the nature of the game and the wording of the Rules.

INTERFERING WITH PLAYERS.

RULE 1.—No player or other person shall be permitted to interfere with the result of a game by any word or act calculated to embarrass the player, nor shall any one, except a partner, speak to a player while in the act of shooting.

ORDER OF COLORS.

RULE 2.—The order of colors shall be red, white, blue, black.

MALLETS.

RULE 3.—There shall be no restriction as to kind or size of mallet used—one or two hands may be used in striking.

RULE 4.—No player shall change his mallet during a game without permission of his opponent, except in case of accident, or to make a "jump shot."

RULE 5.—Should a ball or mallet break in striking, the player may demand another stroke, with a new ball or mallet.

CLIPS OR MARKERS.

RULE 6.—Every player shall be provided with a clip or indicator of the same color as his ball, painted on one side only, which he must affix to his arch next in order in course of play, before his partner plays, with the painted side towards the front of the arch. Should he fail to do so his clip must remain upon the arch it rested on before he played, and he must make the points again. Should he move his marker beyond or back of the point he is for, his attention must be called to such error before he plays again, otherwise it shall stand. Should a player put a ball through its arch, he must move the corresponding clip to its proper arch before the next ball is played, otherwise the clip remains as before. No player shall lose any point or points by the misplacing of his clip by his adversary.

OPENING OF GAME.

RULE 7.—All games shall be opened by scoring from an imaginary line through the middle wicket, and playing two balls each (not partner balls) towards the home stake. The player whose ball rests nearest the stake shall have choice of play, using that ball. The balls shall then be placed in the four corners of the ground (nearest the centre of the field), partner balls diagonally to each other, the playing ball and next in sequence to be placed at the head of the grounds, all balls being in play.

BALLS.—HOW STRUCK.

RULE 8.—The ball must be struck with the face of the mallet, the stroke being delivered whenever touching the ball it moves it. Should a stake or wire intervene, the stroke is not allowed unless the ball is struck at the same time, and if the ball is moved, without being struck by the face of the mallet, it shall remain where it rests, and should a point or roquet be made, it shall not be allowed, except by the decision of the umpire as to the fairness of the shot. All balls thus moved by a false shot may be replaced or not at the option of the opponent.

RULE 9.—When making a direct shot (*i. e.* roquet), the player must not push or follow the ball with his mallet; but when taking croquet from a ball (two balls being in contact), he may follow his ball with the mallet; but must not strike it twice.

RULE 10.—If a player strikes his ball before his opponent has finished his play, the stroke shall stand, or be made over, at the option of the opponent.

RULE 11.—Should a ball rest against or near a wire, and the umpire, or other person agreed on, should decide that in order to pass through the arch, an unfair or push shot would have to be made, it shall not be allowed if made.

FOUL STROKE.

RULE 12.—Should a player in making a stroke move with his mallet any other than his object ball, it shall be a foul and his play ceases, and all balls moved shall be replaced as before the stroke, or remain where they rest, at the option of the opponent.

RULE 13.—If a dead ball in contact with another ball moves, on account of the inequality of the ground, while playing the other ball away from it, the player does not lose his shot.

BALLS.—WHEN NOT TO BE TOUCHED.

RULE 14.—A ball must not be touched while on the field, except after a roquet, when it is necessary to place it beside the roqueted ball for the purpose of croquet, or to replace it when it has been moved by accident—except by permission of the opponent.

ROQUET AND CROQUET.

RULE 15.—A ball roquets another when it comes in contact with it by a blow from the player's mallet, or rebounds from a wicket or a stake or the border; also when it comes in contact with it when croquet is taken from another ball.

RULE 16.—A player after making roquet shall not stop his ball for the purpose of preventing its hitting another. Should he do so his play ceases and all balls shall be replaced as before the stroke, or remain, at the option of the opponent.

RULE 17.—Roquet gives to the player the privilege of roquet-croquet only, and play must be made from the roqueted ball.

RULE 18.—If a player in taking a croquet from a ball, fails to move it, such stroke ends his play, and his ball must be returned, or left where it stops, at the option of the opponent.

RULE 19.—A player, in each turn of play, is at liberty to roquet any ball on the ground once only before making a point.

RULE 20.—Should a player croquet a ball he has not roqueted, he loses his turn, and all balls moved by such play must be replaced to the satisfaction of the umpire, or adversary. Should the mistake not be discovered before the player has made another stroke, the play shall be valid, and the player continue his play.

RULE 21.—In taking croquet from a ball, if player's ball strikes another, to which he is dead, such stroke does not end his play.

RULE 22.—If a player roquets two or more balls at the same stroke, only the first can be croqueted.

MAKING OF POINTS.

RULE 23.—A player makes a point in the game when his ball makes an arch or hits a stake in proper play.

RULE 24.—If a player makes a point, and afterwards at the same stroke roquets a ball, he must take the point, and use the ball. If the roqueted ball is beyond the arch, as determined by rule 45, and playing ball rests through the arch, the arch is held to be first made.*

RULE 25.—If a ball roquets another, and afterwards at the same stroke makes a point, it must take the ball and reject the point.

RULE 26.—A player continues to play so long as he makes a point in the game, or roquets another ball to which he is in play.

RULE 27.—A ball making two or more points at the same stroke, has only the same privilege as if it made but one.

RULE 28.—Should a ball be driven through its arch, or against its stake by croquet or concussion, it is a point made by that ball, except it be a rover. [See Rule 52.]

---

* NOTE.—While this is not mathematically correct, the rule is so made to avoid disputes and difficult measurements.

PLAYING ON DEAD BALL.

RULE 29.—If a player play by direct shot on a dead ball, all balls displaced by such shot shall be replaced in their former position, and the player's ball placed against the dead ball on the side from which it came; or all balls shall rest where they lie, at the option of the opponent.

RULE 30.—If a player, in making a direct shot, strike a ball on which he has already played, *i. e.*, a dead ball, his play ceases. Any point or part of a point or ball struck, after striking the dead ball, is not allowed, and both balls must be replaced in accordance with the preceding rule. A dead ball displaced by other than direct shot, shall not be replaced.

RULE 31.—If playing ball in passing through its arch strike a dead ball that is beyond the arch, as determined by rule 45, the ball shall not be considered a dead ball if playing ball rests through its arch, and the point shall be allowed.

BALLS MOVED OR INTERFERED WITH BY ACCIDENT OR DESIGN.

RULE 32.—A ball accidentally displaced, otherwise than as provided for in Rule 12, must be returned to its position before play can proceed.

RULE 33.—If a ball is stopped or diverted from its course by an opponent, the player may repeat the shot or not as he chooses. Should he decline to repeat the shot, the ball must remain where it stops, and, if playing ball, must play from there.

RULE 34.—If a ball is stopped or diverted from its course by a player or his partner, the opponent may demand a repetition of the shot if he chooses. Should he decline to do so, the ball must remain where it stops, and, if playing ball, must play from there.

RULE 35.—If a ball is stopped or diverted from its course by any object inside the ground, not pertaing to the game or ground, other than provided for in Rules 33 and 34, the shot may be repeated or allowed to remain, at the option of the player. If not repeated, the ball must remain where it stops, and, if playing ball, play from there.

BALLS IN CONTACT.

RULE 36.—Should a player, on commencing his play, find his ball in contact with another, he may hit his own as he likes, and then have subsequent privileges the same as though the balls were separated an inch or more.

RULES CONCERNING BOUNDARY.

[The boundary is a line extending around the field, 30 in. from the border, and parallel with it.]

RULE 37.—A ball shot over boundary or border must be returned at right angles from where it stops.

RULE 38.—A ball is in the field only when the whole ball is within the boundary line.

RULE 39.—No play is allowed from beyond the boundary line, except when a ball is placed in contact with another for the purpose of croquet.

RULE 40.—If a player strikes his ball when over the boundary line, he shall lose his stroke, and the balls shall be replaced or left where they stop, at the option of the opponent.

RULE 41.—If a player hit a ball off the field by a direct shot, his play ceases, and the roqueted ball is placed on the boundary opposite the point where it lay before being thus hit. But if a ball off the field is hit from a croquet, the hit shall not be allowed, the ball shall be replaced properly in the field, and the play shall not cease.

[NOTE.—The three following rules apply more particularly to the old style of grounds with square corners, and are retained for some clubs that have not adopted the new style of grounds.]

RULE 42.—The first ball driven over the boundary line into a corner must be placed on the corner at the intersection of the two boundary lines.

RULE 43.—If a ball, having been struck over the boundary line, is returnable at the corner, another ball being on or entitled to the corner, it shall be placed on that side of the corner ball on which it went off.

RULE 44.—If two balls, having been shot over the boundary line, rest directly behind one another at right angles with boundary line, they shall be placed on the line along side of each other in the same relative position in which they were played off. This can occur only when the centers of the two balls rest directly behind one another at right angles with the boundary line.

BALL.—WHEN THROUGH AN ARCH.

RULE 45.—A ball is not through an arch when a straight edge, laid across the two wires on the side from which the ball came, touches the ball without moving the arch.

BALLS WHEN IN POSITION.

RULE 46.—If a ball has been placed under an arch, for the purpose of croquet, it is not in position to run that arch.

RULE 47.—If a ball be driven under its arch from the wrong direction, and rests there, it is not in position to run that arch in the right direction.

RULE 48.—If a ball, shot through its arch in the right direction, not having come in contact with another ball or the border, rolls back through or under that arch, the point is not made, but the ball is in position if left there.

HITTING BALL WHILE MAKING WICKET.

RULE 49.—The cage wicket may be made in one, two or more turns, provided the ball stops within limit of the cage.

RULE 50.—Any playing ball within, or under, a wicket, becomes dead to advancement through the wicket from that position. if it comes in contact with any other ball by a direct shot.

ROVERS.

RULE 51.—A rover has the right of roquet and consequent croquet on every ball once during each turn of play, and is subject to roquet and croquet by any ball in play.

RULE 52.—Rovers must be continued in the game until partners become rovers, and go out successively, and a rover that has been driven against the stake cannot be removed to make way for the next rover.

PLAYING OUT OF TURN, OR WRONG BALL.

RULE 53 —If a player plays out of his proper turn, whether with his own or any other ball, or in his proper turn plays the wrong ball, and the mistake is discovered before the next player has commenced his play, all benefit from any point or points made is lost, and his turn of play is forfeited. All balls moved by the misplay must be returned to their former position by the umpire or adversary. If the mistake is not discovered until after the next player has made his first stroke, the error must stand.

POINTS RE-MADE.

RULE 54.—If a player makes a point he has already made, his marker not being on that point, and the mistake is discovered before the proper point is made, the play ceases with the shot by which the wicket was re-made, and the marker remains where it stood at the beginning of this play. All balls shall be left in the position they had at the time the wicket was re-made. If not discovered before the proper point is made, the points so made are good, and play proceeds the same as if no error had been made.

ERROR IN ORDER OF PLAY.

RULE 55.—If an error in order is discovered after a player has struck his ball, he shall be allowed to finish his play, provided he is playing in the regular sequence of his partner's ball last played. In case of dispute as to proper sequence of balls, it shall be decided by the umpire; if there is no umpire, by lot. No recourse shall be had to lot unless each party expresses the belief that the other is wrong.

RULE 56.—At any time an error in order is discovered, the opposite side shall follow with the same ball last played (the proper sequence); but before playing, their opponents shall have privilege to demand a transposition of adversaries' balls.

EXAMPLE.—B'ack plays by mistake after Red—the error is not discovered—Blue plays in the proper sequence of his partner Red, and seeing that Black has just played, is thus led to believe it the innocent ball, and upon concluding his play, leaves Black by Red. Now, if error in order is discovered, the player of Red and Blue can demand that the position of Black and White be transposed.

CHANGING SURFACE OF GROUND.

RULE 57.—The surface of grounds shall not be changed during a game by either player, unless by consent of the umpire, and if so changed at the time of playing, the shot shall be declared lost.

DIRECTION THROUGH WICKETS.

RULE 58.—In making all side or corner wickets the playing ball shall pass through them towards the center.

PENALTY.—GENERAL RULE.

RULE 59.—If a rule is violated, a penalty for which has not been provided, the player shall cease his play.

The Association at their meeting in August, 1894, adopted the following:

Should a ball be resting in a corner and another ball be played so that it should be brought in at the same place, it must be placed on that side of the ball upon which it passed over the boundary line.

TOURNAMENT RULES.

RULE 1.—The tournament games shall be played in accordance with the rules of the National Croquet Association.

RULE 2.—No player shall be allowed to enter after 8 o'clock Wednesday morning, except by consent of the Committe of Arrangements.

RULE 3.—All players are expected to remain till the finish and play all games assigned to them; should any player leave before he has played all his games, his unplayed games shall be forfeited, and the Committee of Arrangements shall so record them.

RULE 4.—The order of play shall be determined by lot, names being drawn by the Committee of Arrangements.

RULE 5.—Should any player fail to be present when his turn comes, the next in order shall play, and the former's game be forfeited, unless excused by the Committee of Arrangements.

RULE 6.—All disputed points shall be referred to an umpire, to be chosen before play by the contestants, and in case of his inability to decide, to three referees, to be chosen by the Committee of Arrangements.

RULE 7.—Games shall be called by 8 A.M., and no game shall be begun after 6 P.M., unless by mutual consent.

RULE 8.—All ties shall be played off in accordance with the above rules.

RULE 9.—In case of darkness coming on during a game, the umpire shall decide when a game shall stop, and if stopped, shall be continued first in order the next morning, if the players are on time.

RULE 10.—The players shall be divided into three classes.

The social tournament games will be governed by the same rules as the prize tournament games.

arrangements for special attractions and promote public interest and attendance. They shall also appoint three referees to act during the tournament.

ARTICLE VI.
COMMITTEE ON GROUNDS.

It shall be the duty of this committee to see that all the grounds are put in perfect condition prior to the tournament week, to see that there are a sufficient number of balls and clips, and to generally superintend the many details incident to the care of the grounds.

ARTICLE VII.
FINANCE COMMITTEE.

It shall be the duty of this committee to audit the Treasurer's accounts each year and report the same at the annual meeting; to report as early as possible the probable financial condition of the Association, and in case of a deficiency to provide for the same that all bills may be promptly met.

ARTICLE VIII.
ANNUAL MEETING.

The annual meeting of the Association shall be held the third Tuesday evening in August, at 8 o'clock, in the club house. Special meetings may be called by the President when he may deem it necessary.

ARTICLE IX.
CONSTITUTING A QUORUM.

A majority of the members of the Association shall constitute a quorum at all meetings.

ARTICLE X.
QUESTIONS AND ELECTIONS.

All questions and elections shall be decided by a majority vote.

ARTICLE XI.
FILLING VACANCIES.

The President shall be authorized to fill any vacancy among the officers that occurs through removal or otherwise.

ARTICLE XII.
AMENDMENTS.

These By-Laws may be amended at any annual meeting by a vote of two-thirds of the members of the Association present.

PAST OFFICERS.

The following are the past officers of the Association.

1882.
Pres.—Ira B. Read, M.D., N. Y.; Vice-Pres.—J. W. Hooker, Norwich, Conn.; Sec. and Treas.—Geo. W. Johnson, Phila., Penn.; Cor. Sec'y—C. H. Botsford, N. Y.

1883.
Pres.—Geo. W. Johnson, Phila., Penn.; Vice-Pres.—G. Maurer, Keyport, N. J.; Rev Philip Germond, N. Y.; John M. Brewer, Norwich, Conn.; M. Driver, Staten Island; Sec'y and Treas.—A. W. Dickey, Norwich, Conn.; Cor. Sec'y—C. H. Bottsford, N. Y.

1884.
Pres.—A. W. Dickey, Norwich, Conn.; Vice-Pres.—P. B. Ashley, Providence, R. I.; J. DeGolyer, Troy, N. Y.; S. D. Warrener, New London, Conn.; Sec'y and Treas.—Prof. Charles Jacobus, Springfield, Mass; Cor. Sec'y—C H. Botsford, N. Y.

1885.
Pres.—Prof. Charles Jacobus, Springfield, Mass.; Vice-Pres.—W. W. Whitman, Troy, N. Y.; E. M. Baldwin, Danbury, Conn.; Dr. Davenport, Northampton, Mass.; Sec'y and Treas.—N. L. Bishop, Norwich, Conn.; Cor. Sec'y—C. H. Botsford, N. Y.

1886.
Pres.—W. W. Whitman, Troy; Vice-Pres.—J. W. Tuffts, Boston; L. P. Bryant Northampton, Mass.; Chas. H. Bush, Staten Island; Rec. Sec'y and Treas.—C. H. Pettis, Norwich; Acting Sec'y and Treas.—N. L. Bishop, Norwich; Cor. Sec'y—C. H. Botsford, N. Y.

1887.
Pres.—E. M. Barnum, Danbury, Conn.; Vice-Pres.—Frank Sisson, New London, Conn.; T. A. Harris, Philadelphia; C A. Marsh, New York; Sec'y and Treas.—N. L. Bishop, Norwich; Cor. Sec'y—C. H. Botsford, N. Y.

1888.

Pres.—A. W. Wambold, Staten Island; Vice-Pres.—Geo. C. Strong, New London, Conn.; Geo. Van Wickle, New Brunswick, N. J.; E. F. Spalding, Townsend Harbor, Mass.; Sec'y and Treas.—N. L. Bishop, Norwich, Conn.; Cor. Sec'y, L. P. Bryant, Florence, Mass.

1889.

Pres.—Herbert Porter, Malden, Mass.; Vice-Pres.—John M. Brewer, Norwich; Abner B. Holley, New York; Joseph Bilbrough, Philadelphia; Sec'y and Treas.—Charles Jacobus, Springfield, Mass.; Cor. Sec'y—A. W. Dickey, Norwich.

1890.

Pres—John M. Brewer, Norwich; Vice-Pres.—Abner B. Holley, New York; Joseph Bilbrough, Philadelphia; J. W. Tufts, Boston; Sec'y and Treas.—Charles Jacobus, Springfield, Mass.; Cor. Sec'y—George W. Johnson, Philadelphia, Pa.

1891.

Pres.—John M. Brewer, Norwich; Vice-Pres.—E. R. Downs. Asbury Grove; John P. Dechen, Staten Island; E. C. Butler, Middletown; Sec'y and Treas—Charles Jacobus, Springfield, Cor. Sec'y—George W. Johnson, Philadelphia, Pa.

1892.

Pres.—N. L. Bishop, Norwich; Vice-Pres.—C. S. Myers, Washington, D. C.; D. B. Frisbee, New York; L. G. Williams, Mansfield Centre, Conn.; Sec'y and Treas.—Charles Jacobus, Springfield, Mass.; Cor. Sec'y—W. Holt Apgar, Trenton, N. J.

1893.

Pres.—George C. Strong, New London; Vice-Pres.—William Holden, Leominster, Mass.; G. Maurer, Keyport, N. J.; Charles Greenslit, Philadelphia; Sec'y and Treas.—Dale D. Butler, Middletown, Conn.; Cor. Sec'y—H. G. Fay, Brooklyn, N. Y.

1894.

Pres.—Henry G. Fay, Brooklyn, N. Y.; Vice-Pres.—G. S. Burgess, Lynn, Mass.; Jas. B. Hickman, Wilmington, Del.; W. S. Chase, Washington, D. C.; Sec'y and Treas.—N. L. Bishop, Norwich, Conn.; Cor. Sec'y—Philip Germond, New York, N. Y.

1895.

Pres.—Abner B. Holley, New York ; Vice-Pres.—W. Holt Apgar, Trenton. N. J.; W. A. Towne, New London, Conn.; W. H. Wahley, Washington, D. C.; Sec'y and Treas.—N. L. Bishop, Norwich, Conn.

1896.

Pres.—Geo. S. Van Wickle, New Brunswick, N.J.; Vice-Pres.—E. M. Baldwin, Danbury, Conn.; H. Wahley, Washington, D.C., and Frank Sisson, New London, Conn.; Sec'y and Treas.—N. L. Bishop, Norwich, Conn.

THE SPALDING CUP OF 1890-91.

The prizes awarded to Mr. Gustavus Maurer for shortest game, for two years, by A. G. Spalding & Bros., were condensed into one unique and valuable Cup. This stands about twelve inches high, and at the same time attests the *interest of those who awarded* it, the *skill of the artist* in manufacture, and the *rapidly delicate croquet playing* of Mr. Maurer.

THE GEO. S. VAN WICKLE BADGE.

A gold badge has been presented by George S. Van Wickle to the Association, to be contested for by the clubs of the Association, and the following rules, to govern these contests, have been adopted:

The badge to be held by the individual winner, subject to challenge once a month, on seven days' notice, by a member selected to play for it by any club belonging to the National Association. No club shall have a right to a second challenge in less than ninety days from the first. The games to be best four in seven, and must be played on grounds chosen by the person holding the badge.

NOTE.—First Contest—At Philadelphia, Fall Tournament, October 3, 1891; won by G. W. Johnson. Second Contest—At Philadelphia, June, 1892; held by Johnson vs. Germond. Third Contest—At Norwich, August, 1892; won by Jacobus. Fourth Contest—At Springfield, October, 1892; held by Jacobus vs. Germond. Fifth Contest—At Springfield, 1893; won by L. P. Bryant. Sixth Contest—At Cottage City, 1895; won by Chas. Jacobus and given up to George C Strong without contest in 1896. Eighth Contest—At Norwich, 1896; held by Strong vs. W. H. Wahley.

☞ By vote of Association, the contest for this badge wil take place annually at Norwich during tournament week.

PRIZE WINNERS.

1882.
1st.—A. G. SHIPMAN..New York
2d. —IRA B. READ..New York

1883.
1st.—G. W. JOHNSON...Philadelphia
2d. —IRA B. READ..New York

1884.
1st.—GEN. HARLAND...Norwich
2d. —CHARLES JACOBUS...Springfield

1885.
1st.—CHARLES JACOBUS...Springfield
2d. —C. HULL BOTSFORD..New York

1886.
1st.—C. HULL BOTSFORD..New York
2d. —CHARLES JACOBUS...Springfield

1887.
1st.—A. WAMBOLD...Staten Island
2d. —CHARLES JACOBUS...Springfield

1888.
1st.—N. L. BISHOP..Norwich
2d. —L. P. BRYANT...Florence, Mass.

1889.
1st.—G. W. JOHNSON...Philadelphia
2d. —CHARLES JACOBUS...Springfield

1890.
1st.—GEORGE C. STRONG......................................New London
2d. —Was tied for by NASH, WAMBOLD and CHAS. JACOBUS and not played off.

1891.
1st.—CHARLES G. SMITH....................................Martha's Vineyard
2d. —PHILIP GERMOND..New York

1892.

FIRST DIVISION.

1ST.—G. W. JOHNSON.................................... Philadelphia
2D. — GEORGE C. STRONG............................... New London

1893.

FIRST DIVISION.

1ST.—W. KNECHT..... .... Matawan, N. J.
2D.—PHILIP GERMOND..................................... New York

1894.

FIRST DIVISION.

1ST. –GEORGE C. STRONG .... New London
2D. –PHILIP GERMOND..................................... New York

SECOND DIVISION.

1ST.—GEORGE S. BURGESS............................... Lynn, Mass.
2D. —HENRY G. FAY .... Brooklyn, N. Y.

THIRD DIVISION.

1ST.—W. A. TOWNE.. New London
2D. —Was tied for by DR. DAVENPORT, C. M. BRYANT and T. W. WHITE. By vote the Association awarded Dr. Davenport second prize, the other contestants not appearing to play off the tie.

1895.

FIRST DIVISION.

1ST.—GEORGE C. STRONG..... .... New London
2D. —GEORGE S. BURGESS............ Asbury Grove Club, Lynn, Mass.

SECOND DIVISION.

TIED FOR BOTH PRIZES.
- HENRY G. FAY............................... Brooklyn, N. Y.
- W. H. WAHLEY...... .... Washington, D. C.
- W. HOLT APGAR................................. Trenton, N. J.

AUGUST 17 AND 18, 1896—TIES PLAYED OFF.
1ST.—W. H. WAHLEY................................. Washington, D. C.
2D. —W. HOLT APGAR................................. Trenton, N. J.

THIRD DIVISION.

1ST.—W. C. CADY... New London
2D. —A. B. SMITH....................................... Northampton

1896.

FIRST DIVISION.

1ST.—EARLE C. BUTLER......................... Middletown, Conn.
2D. —FRANK SISSON............................. New London, Conn.

SECOND DIVISION.

1ST.—FRED S. JANES............................ New London, Conn.
2D. —J. N. DAVENPORT......................... Northampton, Mass.

SPALDING'S FINE CROQUET.

Expert Sets.

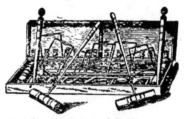

		Set.
No. A.	Lakeside Set, four Mallets and Balls	$3.00
No. B.	Hyde Park Set, four Mallets and Balls	5.00
No. D.	Staten Island Set, four Boxwood Mallets and Balls	10.00
No. E.	Staten Island Set, eight Boxwood Mallets and Balls	15.00
No. G.	Expert Set, four Mallets and Balls	25.00

Practice Sets.

No. 1.	Eight Ball Set, Flat Box	1.00
No. 2.	Eight Ball Set, Large Mallet Heads	1.50
No. 3.	Eight Ball Set, Larger Mallet Heads	2.00
No. 4.	Eight Ball Set, Extra Large Mallet Heads	3.00

Expert Mallets.

No. 1.	"Tuxedo Club" Mallet, 18 and 24-inch handles	3.00
No. 2.	"The Expert" Mallet, 12 and 18-inch handles	3.00
No. 5.	"Club Special" Mallet, 18 or 24-inch handle....Each,	1.50
No. 7.	"The Club" Mallet, 18 or 24-inch handle "	1.25

Balls.

No. 0.	Finest Hard Rubber...................Each,	2.50
No. 1.	Finest Lignum-vitæ "	.75
No. 3.	Composition Rubber Balls "	.75
No. 4.	Dogwood Balls "	.50

Lawn Bowls.

Complete Sets in Box.   Set.

No. 3 Set.	Bowls 4½ in. diameter	$8.00
No. 4 Set.	Bowls 5 in. diameter	10.00
No. 5 Set.	Bowls extra large	12.00

Handsomely Illustrated Catalogue Free.

New York   **A. G. SPALDING & BROS.**,   Philadelphia
Chicago   Washington

 Highest Quality
WOOD CLUBS

Are made of the finest, clear, selected dogwood, persimmon or compressed hickory, and are finished entirely by hand by expert Scotch club n.akers.

 Highest Quality
IRON CLUBS

Are all hand-hammered from the finest dropped forgings, and are patterns of the favorite clubs used by the leading amateurs and professionals. The unanimous verdict of the best players in the country is that they have no superior. They are fully guaranteed.

"The Spalding," any style................................Each, **$2.25**
"The Spalding Special," any style...................... "   **1.50**
"The Clan" Clubs, any style........................... "   **1.00**

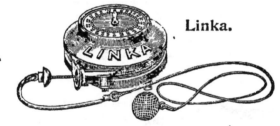

Linka.

The game of Linka gives all an opportunity of enjoying this popular game on any ordinary lawn. The machine is of iron, and when the ball is struck in the ordinary way registers the distance traveled. Complete instructions with each outfit...............Each, **$10.00**

Captive Golf.

Our Complete Golf Ball Outfit will enable the player to practice the different strokes in an ordinary field, and is especially recommended to beginners.

No. 1.   Captive Golf Outfit................................Each, **$1.50**

Putting Golf.

A new Golf Game for Indoor or Outdoor use.   EACH
No. 6. Game complete, with implements......................**$5.00**

Handsomely Illustrated Catalogue Free.

New York   **A. G. SPALDING & BROS.,**   Philadelphia
Chicago   Washington

GOLF SUNDRIES.

Golf Balls.

	Doz
The "Silvertown" Ball	$5.00
The "Henley" Ball	5.00
The Spalding "Highest Quality" Ball	4.00
The "Practice" Ball	2.50

Old Balls Made New.

We have put in a special plant at our factory for the remoulding of old golf balls. These balls are not remoulded in the ordinary way, but undergo the identical process used in making a new ball; the result is a ball about ½ to 1 pennyweight lighter than the original 27 or 27½ ball, but otherwise it is precisely the same as regards looks, durability and elasticity. We can remake and return balls within ten days of receipt and guarantee to do so. Express must be prepaid.........Doz., **$1.25**

Home Golf Ball Press

For Remoulding Damaged Balls.

No. 30. Ball Press.........Each, **$5.00**

Golf Ball Painting Machine.

To hold ball when repainting same.

No. 35. Ball Machine.................Each, **$2.00**

Ball Cleaner.

No. 25. Rubber Case, with Sponge......Each, **75c.**

Macpherson's Golfer's Companion.

For Repainting Balls.

Outfit consists of rack for holding three balls, can of enamel and brush.   Each.

No. 1. Macpherson's Outfit, complete....**$1.00**

Golf Ball Paint.   Per Can.

No. 9. Pierce's, Red or White............**40c.**

Handsomely Illustrated Catalogue Free.

New York   **A. G. SPALDING & BROS.,**   Philadelphia
Chicago   Washington

PRICE LIST
The Christy Anatomical Saddle

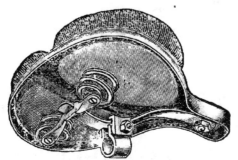

WITH SPIRAL SPRINGS.

No. 1. Men's model, width of seat 8 in., **$5.00**
No. 3. Men's model, width of seat 8¾ in., **5.00**

WITH FLAT SPRINGS.

No. 5. Men's model, width of seat 8 in., **$5.00**
No. 7. Men's model, width of seat 8¾ in., **5.00**

WOMEN'S MODELS.

No. 9. Women's Special Saddle, Spiral Springs, ... **$5.00**
No. 11. Women's Special Saddle, Flat Springs, ... **5.00**

Insist on the Christy Saddle being fitted to your bicycle.
No dealer will lose a sale on account of your preference.

A. G. SPALDING & BROS. New York Chicago
Philadelphia

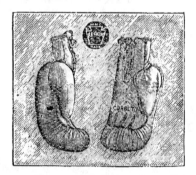

WRIGHT & DITSON

Makers of the

New Pim

...and...

Famous Campbell Rackets

Send for our Complete Illustrated Catalogue

Manufacturers of
Fine Lawn Tennis and Golf Goods

WRIGHT & DITSON'S
Championship ····Ball····

Adopted by the United States Lawn Tennis Association, Intercollegiate Lawn Tennis Association, Southern Lawn Tennis Association, Canadian Lawn Tennis Association, and other Associations of the United States and Canada.

Offices and Salesrooms, 344 Washington St., Boston, Mass.
FACTORY, WAKEFIELD, MASS.

TENNIS SETS.

No. 2. THE FAVORITE SET, consisting of 4 "Favorite" Rackets, 4 rubber balls, 1 net, 27 x 3 feet, 2 portable poles, 1 mallet, 1 set of guy ropes, book of rules; in box complete.
Per set, **$10.00**

No. 3. THE GENEVA SET, consisting of 4 "Geneva" Rackets and rubber balls, 1 net, 27 x 3 feet, 2 portable poles, 1 mallet, 1 set guy ropes, book of rules; in box, complete.
Per set, **$12.50**

No. 4. THE GREENWOOD SET, consisting of 4 "Greenwood" Rackets, 1 net, 33 x 3 feet, four covered balls, 2 portable poles, 1 mallet, 1 set guy ropes, book of rules; in box, complete..........Per set, **$15.00**

No. 5. THE LAKESIDE SET, consisting of 4 "Lakeside" Rackets, 1 net, 33 x 3 feet, 4 covered balls, 2 portable poles, 1 mallet, 1 set of guy ropes, book of rules; in box, complete......................Per set, **$20.00**

No. 8 THE SLOCUM JUNIOR SET, consisting of 4 "Slocum Junior" Rackets, 12 regulation balls, 1 canvas-bound net, 42 x 3 feet, 2 portable poles, 1 mallet, 1 set guy ropes, book of rules; in handsome box, complete...Per set, **$30.00**

No. 9. THE SLOCUM SET, consisting of 4 celebrated "Slocum" Rackets, 12 regulation balls, 1 hand-made canvas-bound net, 42 x 3 feet, poles, guy ropes, rules, all in handsome box, complete....Per set, **$40.00**

No. 11. THE SLOCUM TOURNAMENT SET, consisting of 4 "Slocum Tournament" Rackets, otherwise same as No. 9....Per set, **$50.00**

Wright & Ditson's Official Tennis Guide for 1897.

Containing latest rules, fixtures for 1897, and interesting statistics of the game..Each, **10c**

Dwight's Pocket Score Book.
FOR LAWN TENNIS.

This book is arranged to keep the score of tennis matches in every detail. Leaves perforated, to be torn out if desired................Each, **10c.**

Official Lawn Tennis Score Book.

As adopted by the United States National Lawn Tennis Association. Especially compiled for the use of Tennis Reporters and Official Scorers, by Joseph T. Whittlesey, Secretary U.S.N.L.T.A. Each, **50c.**

"Slocum on Tennis."

Containing 224 pages, with numerous instantaneous photos illustrating services and strokes, and much valuable information for beginners.
Price, paper covers....................................Each, $ **.50**
Price cloth covers...................................... " **1.00**

Handsomely Illustrated Catalogue Free.

New York   **A. G. SPALDING & BROS.,**   Philadelphia
Chicago   Washington

Spalding's Tennis Rackets.

No. 13. *The Spalding* Racket, Frame of finest quality white ash, handsomely polished, the stringing of the highest quality gut and specially made for this Racket, throat-piece of rosewood, handle cane spliced and cane extending through throat-piece, giving additional strength and greatly increasing the resiliency and driving power. It is hand-made throughout and of the finest workmanship, as indicated by our special trade mark of "Highest Quality"..................Each, **$8.00**

❋ ❋ ❋

"Slocum" Rackets.

Extra Fine Quality.

No. 12.
THE SLOCUM OVAL

No. **12.** The "Slocum Oval," finest white ash frame, strung with finest Oriental white gut, new oval-shaped handle, handsomely polished and finished in antique oak, scored sides......... **$7.00**

No. **11.** The "Slocum Tournament," frame and stringing same as in our No. 12 Racket, but handle of regular shape and made of polished mahogany, checkered on all sides and leather capped........................Each, **$7.00**

No. **9.** The "Slocum," frame of selected and polished white ash, Oriental "B" main strings and red cross strings, polished cedar handle, finely checkered, and all of superior quality......**$5.00**

No. **9C.** Same, only with Cork Handle, **$5.50**

No. **8.** The "Slocum Junior," frame of fine white ash, polished cherry throat-piece, checkered cedar handles, strung with all white Oriental **$4.00**

Handsomely Illustrated Catalogue Free.

New York
Chicago **A. G. SPALDING & BROS.,** Philadelphia
Washington

Wright & Ditson's Championship Tennis Ball

For 1897.

No. **5.** W. & D. Ball..........Per doz., **$5.00**

No. **O.** Spalding's Tournament Ball, covered with fine felt and warranted first-class in every particular......................Per doz., **$4.00**

Rubber Handle Covers.

Made of corrugated rubber, for covering racket handles to secure better grip.

No. **1.** Rubber...Each, **25c.**

Racket Presses.

To prevent warping when Ratchet is not in use.

No. **1.** The "Star" Racket Press......Each, **$1.00**

Racket Covers.

No. **1.** Fine Felt Cover.....................Each, **$ .50**
No. **2.** Canvas, leather bound............. " **1.00**
No. **4.** Mackintosh, waterproof............ " **1.00**
No. **5.** Fine Bridle Leather, embossed and shaped to Racket........................ " **4.00**

Restringing Rackets.

Restrung with

Good American Gut, White only..........................Each, **1.25**
Best American Gut, White, Red, or Red and White........ " **1.75**
Fine English Gut, White, Red, or Red and White.......... " **2.75**

Tennis Scorer.

An ingenious device for fastening to Racket for registering the game.
No. **8.** Scorer..Each, **.25**

Handsomely Illustrated Catalogue Free.

New York / Chicago **A. G. SPALDING & BROS.,** Philadelphia / Washington

WHIST

By A. Howard Cady

PUBLISHED BY
The American Sports Publishing Co.
241 BROADWAY, NEW YORK.

ENTERED AT THE NEW YORK POST OFFICE, N.Y., AS SECOND CLASS MATTER.

Model No. 524. **For 1897**

Price, $100

SPECIFICATIONS

FRAME—Diamond, standard height 24 inches, front tubes 1⅛ inch, rear tubes ¾ inch, swaged and tapered at all connections, excepting at crank hanger. All connections, except one, steel thimbles. Tubular construction throughout.

FRONT FORK—Double plate crown. Side forks of large section, reinforced and gracefully tapered. No forgings.

BEARINGS—Tool steel cut from bar, tempered, ground and polished.

TIRES—28 inches by 1⅝ inches. (See Options.)

SPOKES—Straight, tangent, swaged and nickeled.

CRANKS—6¾ inches. Round, spring steel, detachable.

PEDALS—Spalding combination, rubber and rat-trap. Dust proof.

HANDLE BARS—Steel tubing of large section. Cork grips.

BRAKE—Direct plunger with rubber friction blocks. Detachable.

SADDLE—Christy, with "T" post.

GEAR—70 inches—20 teeth by 8 teeth.

FITTINGS—Tool Bag, with tools and repair kit.

WEIGHT—Without brake, 23 pounds.

TREAD—5 inches.

FINISH—Black enamel, nickeled trimmings.

OPTIONS—20-inch frame, Model No. 520; 22-inch frame, Model No. 522; 26-inch frame, Model No. 526; 28-inch frame, Model No. 528; Handle Bars, Nos. 1, 2, 3, 4, 5, 6, 7, 8, 9, 10 (see page 81); Sprockets, front, 17, 18, 19, 20, 21, 22, 23, 24, 25; Sprockets, rear, 8, 9, 10 (for table of gears see page 63); Cranks, 6½, 7, 7½ or 8 inches; Spalding Adjustable Gooseneck Post; Tires, Spaulding & Pepper, Hartford, Palmer, Goodrich Single Tube or Dunlop Detachable; Pedals, extra wide; Saddle, Sager; Finish, dark blue or carmine enamel, gold striped, cherry finished rims.

NOTE—Brake cannot be fitted to handle bars Nos. 3, 4 or 5.

A. G. SPALDING & BROS.

New York   Chicago   Philadelphia

Factory, Chicopee Falls, Mass.

Published Monthly
Price Ten Cents

SPALDING'S HOME LIBRARY

Devoted to Games and Pastimes of Interest to the Home Circle ♣ ♣ ♣

1 Chess
2 Whist
3 Dominoes and Dice
4 Poker
5 Backgammon
6 Euchre
7 Billiards
8 Ecarte
9 Checkers
10 Bezique
11 Pool
12 Pinochle
13 Loto
14 Hearts
15 Reversi
16 Piquet
17 Go-Bang

**American Sports Publishing Company
241 Broadway
New York**

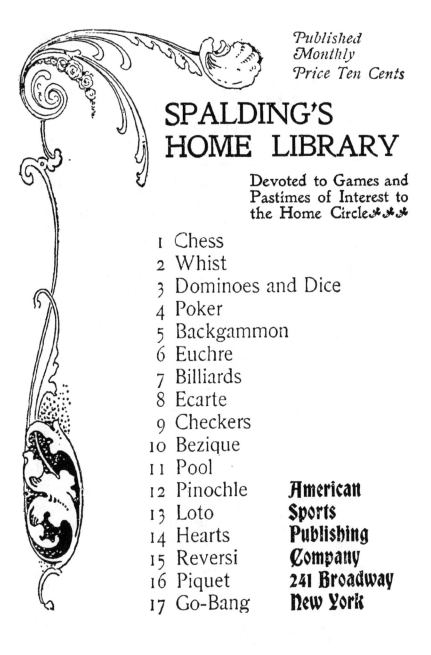

SPALDING'S
Athletic Library

No.   Published Monthly

1. Life and Battles of James J. Corbett.
2. Indian Clubs and Dumb Bells.
4. How to Become a Boxer.
5. Gymnastics. [Campbell.
6. How to Play Lawn Tennis. By Champion
7. How to Play Base Ball. Just the thing for Boys. By Walter Camp.
9. The Athlete's Guide. How to Run, Sprint, Jump, Walk, and Throw Weights.
12. Association Foot Ball.
13. Hand Ball.
14. Curling, Hockey and Polo.
16. Skating. A very practical book. By Champion
18. Fencing. [Geo. D. Phillips.
20. Cricket Guide. By Geo. Wright.
21. Rowing. By E. J. Giannini, Champion Amateur
23. Canoeing. By C. Bowyer Vaux. [Oarsman.
25. Swimming. By Walter G. Douglas.
26. How to Play Foot Ball. By Walter Camp.
27. College Athletics. By M. C. Murphy.
29. Exercising with Pulley Weights. By H. S. Anderson.
30. How to Play Lacrosse. By W. H Corbett.
32. Practical Ball Playing. By Arthur A. Irwin.
36. How to Play Golf. Edited by L. B. Stoddart.
37. All Around Athletics.
39. Lawn Bowls. By Henry Chadwick.
40. Archery. By James S. Mitchel.
42. How to Use the Punching Bag.
50. Spalding's Lawn Tennis Guide.
51. Rowing Guide.
52. Official Croquet Guide.
53. Intercollegiate A. A. A. A. Guide.
54. Official Foot Ball Guide for 1896. Edited by Walter Camp.
55. Sporting Rules; for discus throwing, etc.
56. Official Basket Ball Guide for 1896-7.
57. Official Roller Polo Guide for 1896-7.
58. Bowling. Latest rules and regulations.
59. Official Bicycle Guide. Instructions to cyclists; Portraits of all leading riders; complete list of
60. Indoor Base Ball. [records.
61. Athletic Almanac for 1897.
62. Military Cycling in the Rocky Mountains. By Lieut. James A. Moss, U. S. A.
63. Spalding's Official Base Ball Guide for 1897.

Per Copy, 10 cents, postpaid.

AMERICAN SPORTS PUBLISHING CO.
241 BROADWAY, NEW YORK.

SPALDING'S...
Illustrated Catalogue

Fall and Winter
SPORTS...

Published about August First.

Foot Ball   Ice Skates
Golf and Polo

ATHLETIC AND GYMNASIUM OUTFITS.

Sweaters, Hunting Clothing and Equipments, and all Accessories for Fall and Winter Wear🍀🍀🍀

Handsomely illustrated, and the recognized authority for standard and up-to-date goods. Mailed free to any address.

A. G. Spalding & Bros.

NEW YORK   CHICAGO   PHILADELPHIA

CPSIA information can be obtained
at www.ICGtesting.com
Printed in the USA
LVHW011620091222
734910LV00004B/278